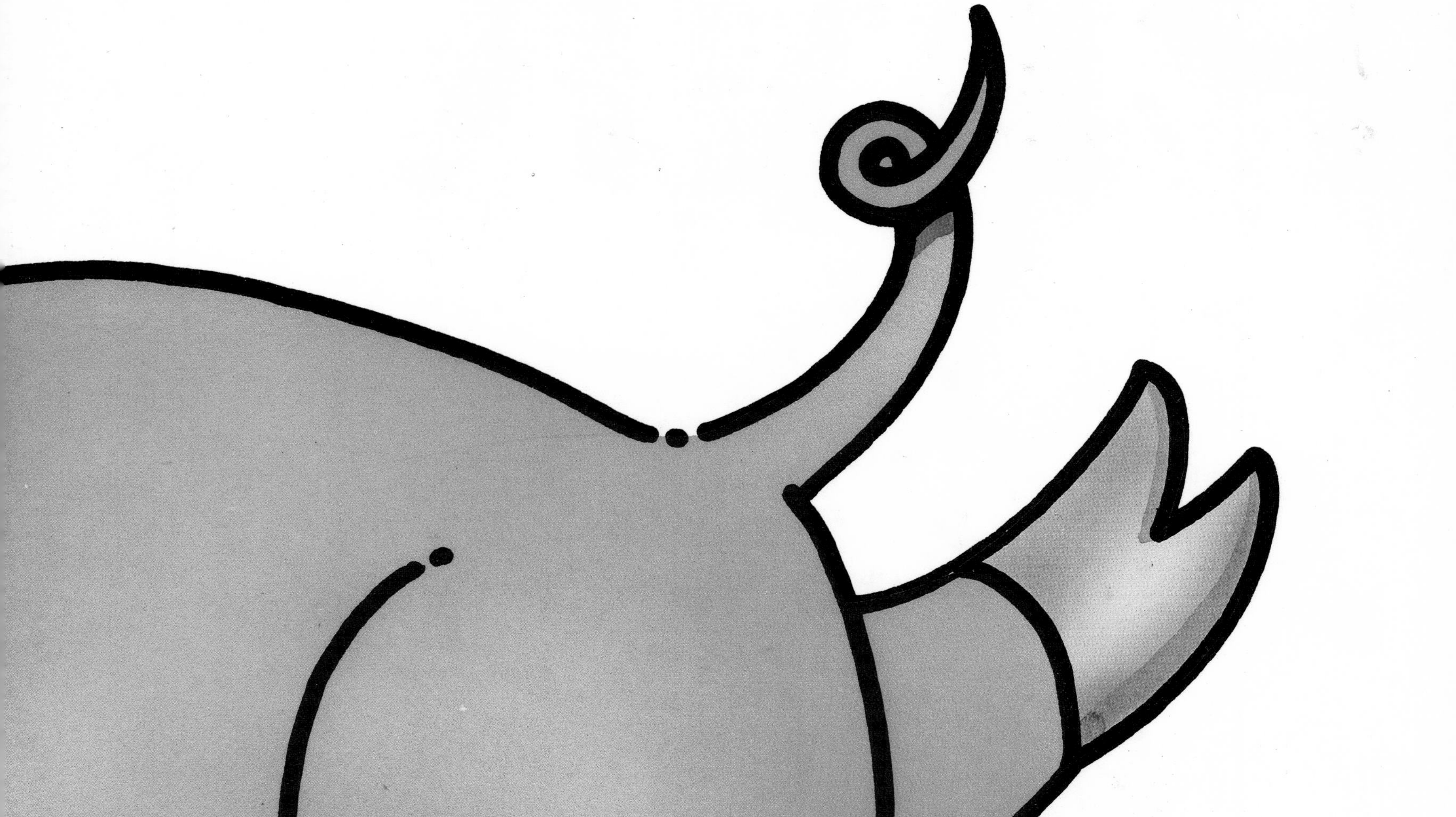

Pig

BLUE

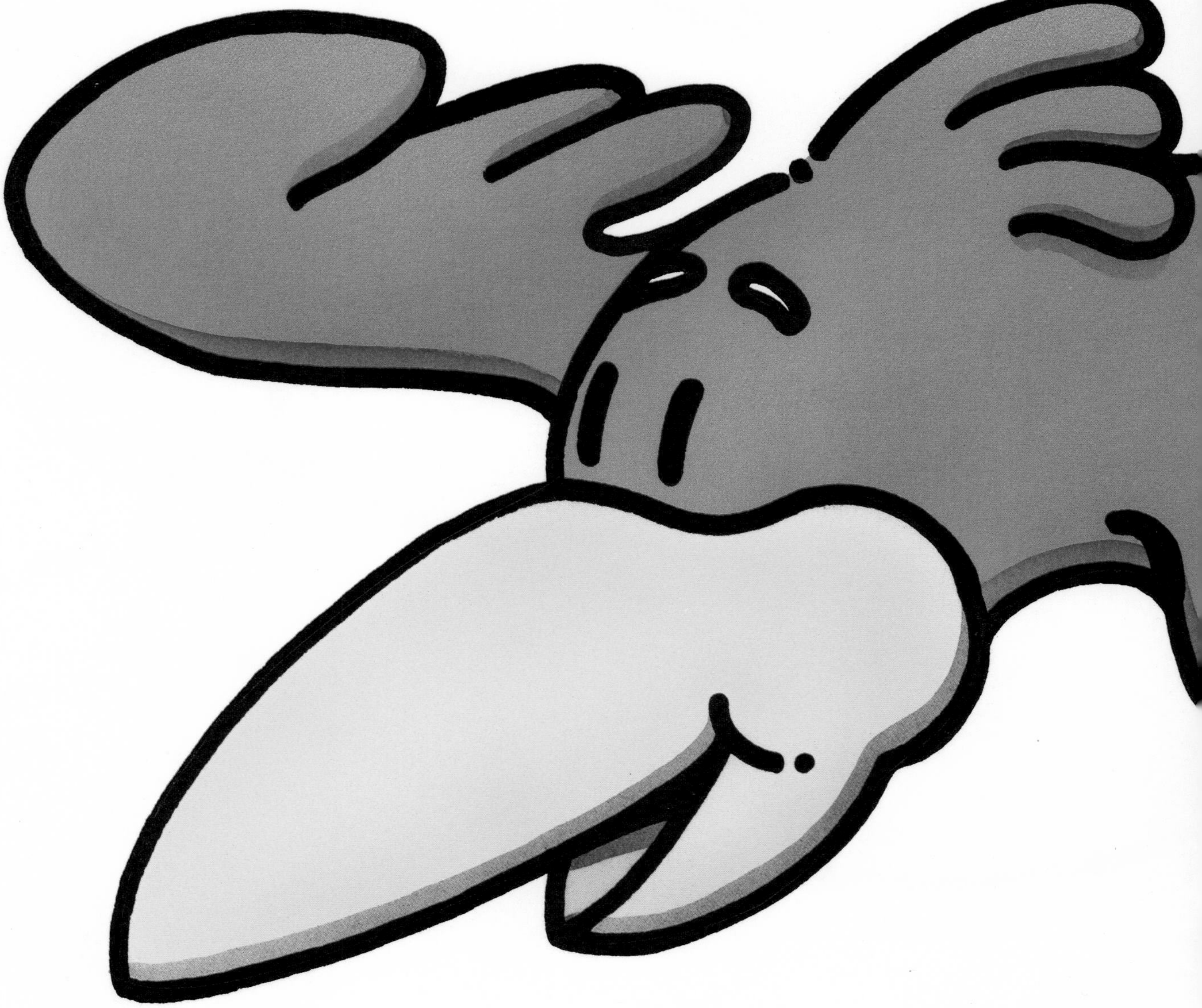

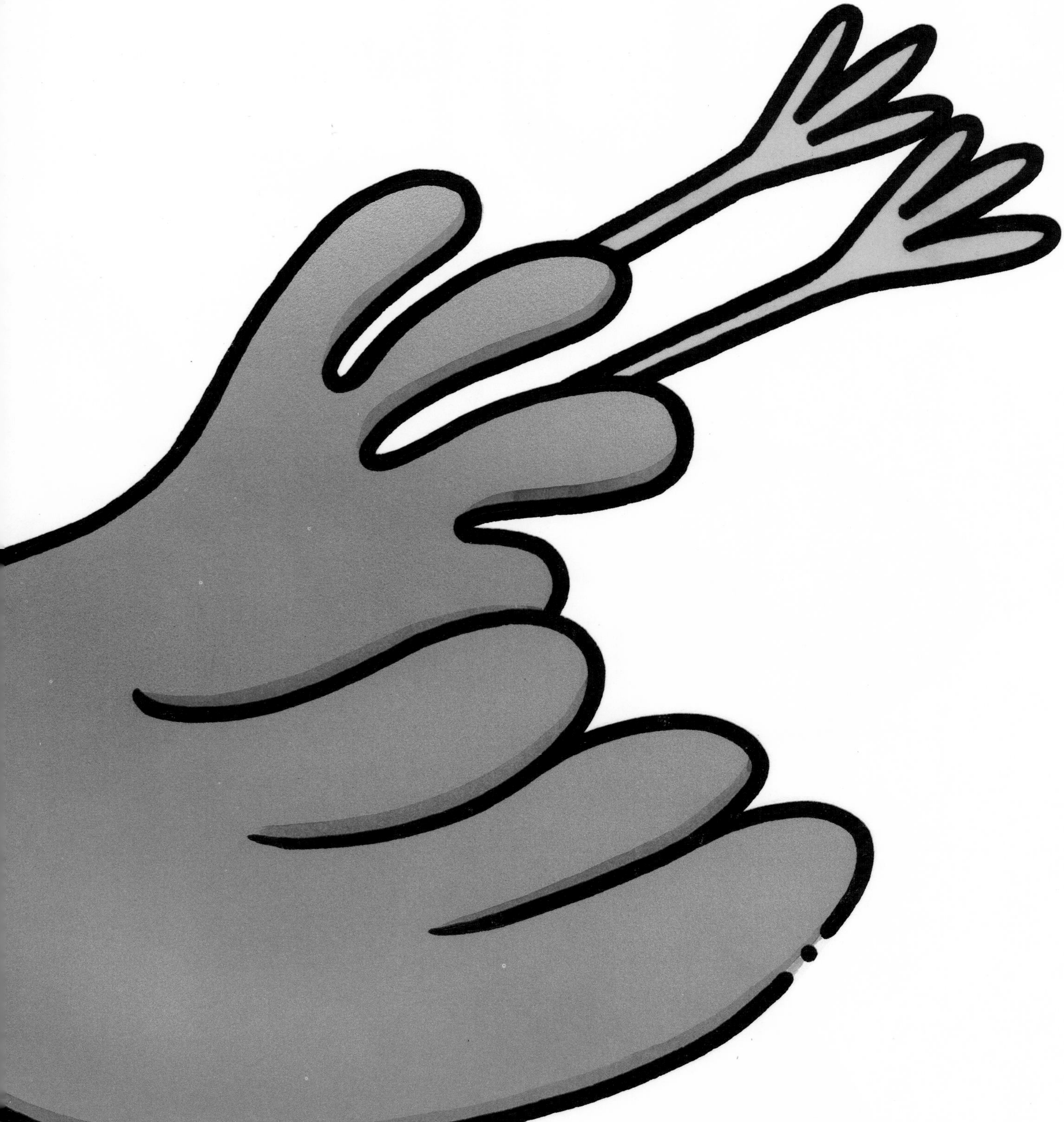

Bird

RED

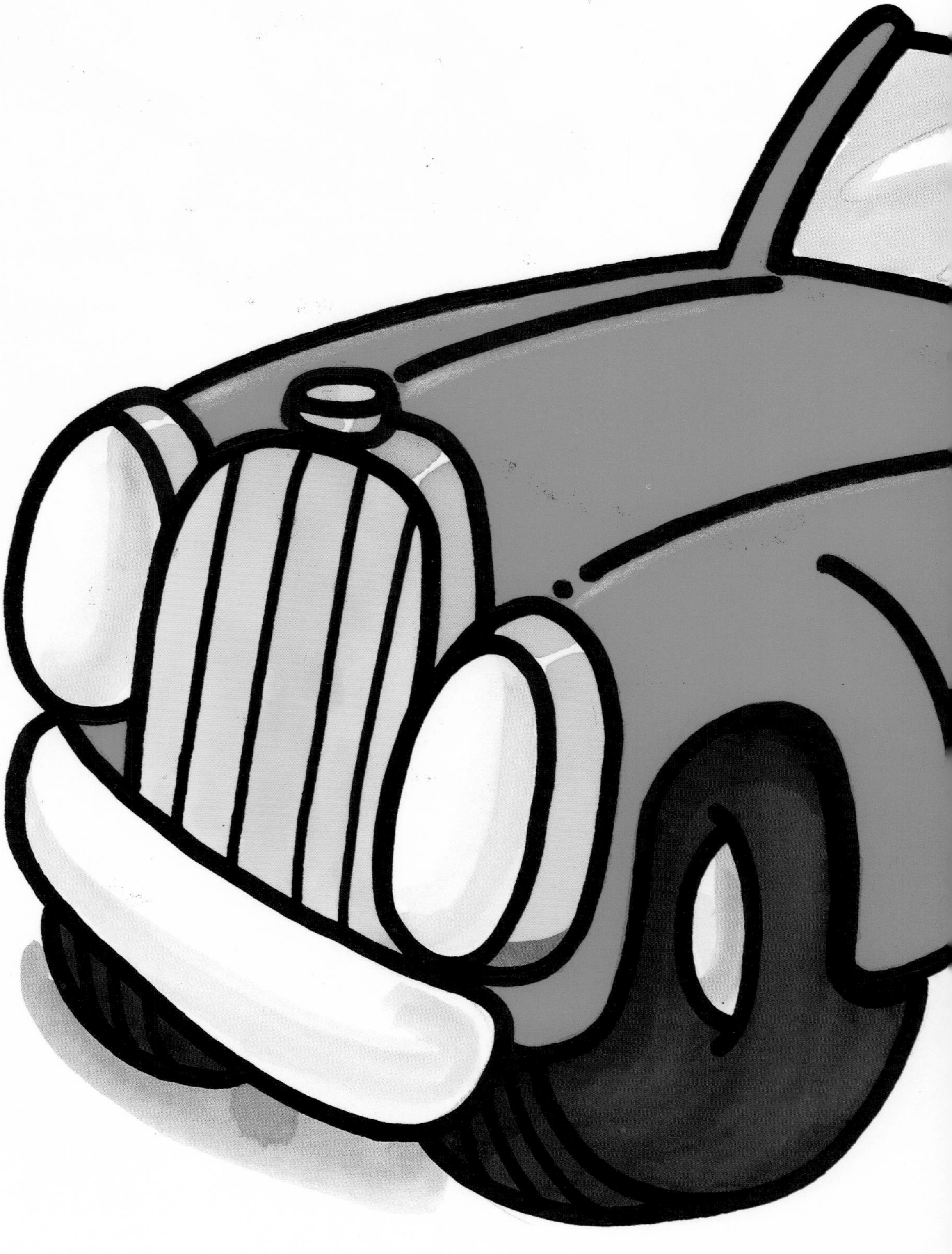

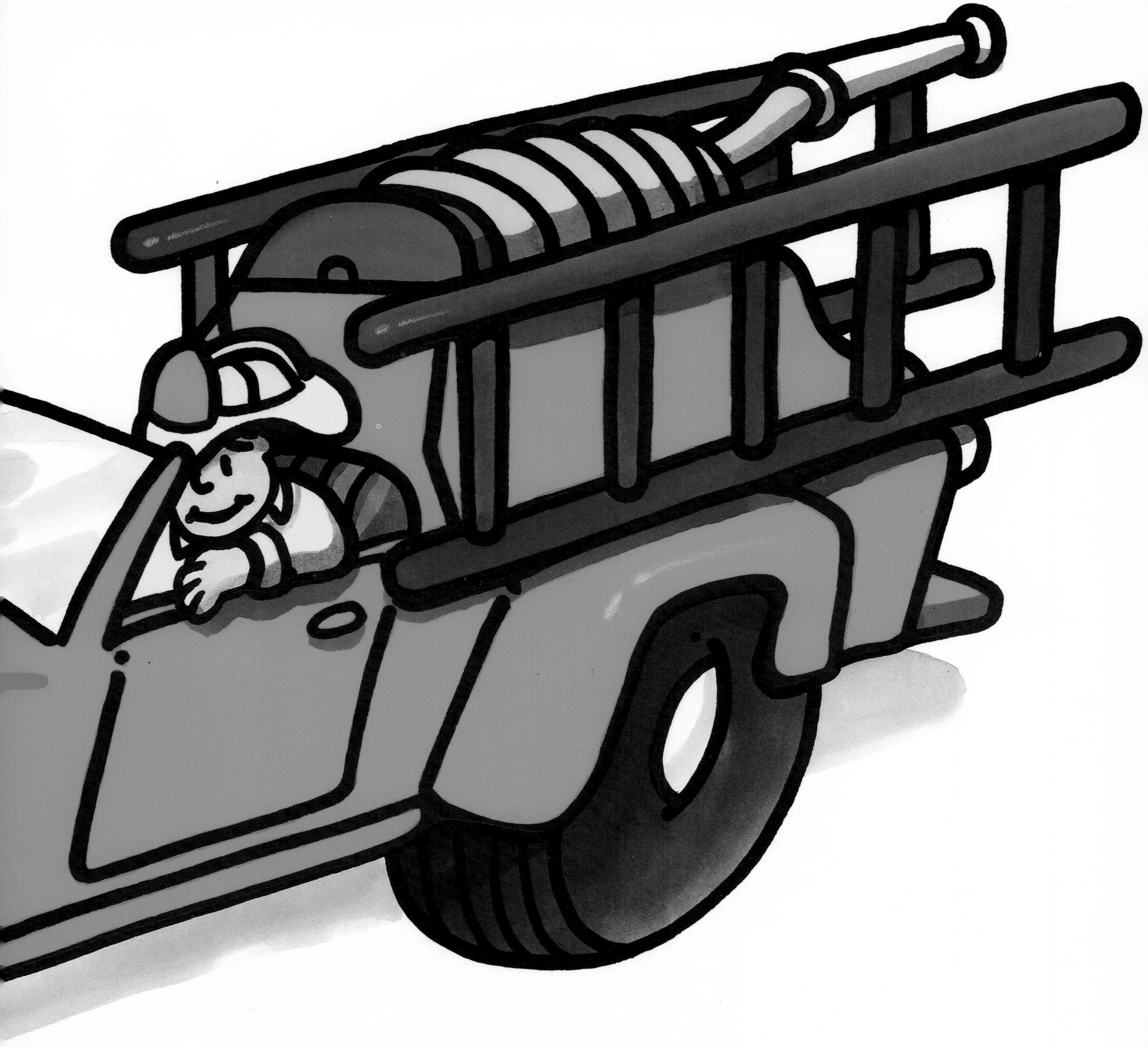

Firetruck

BROW

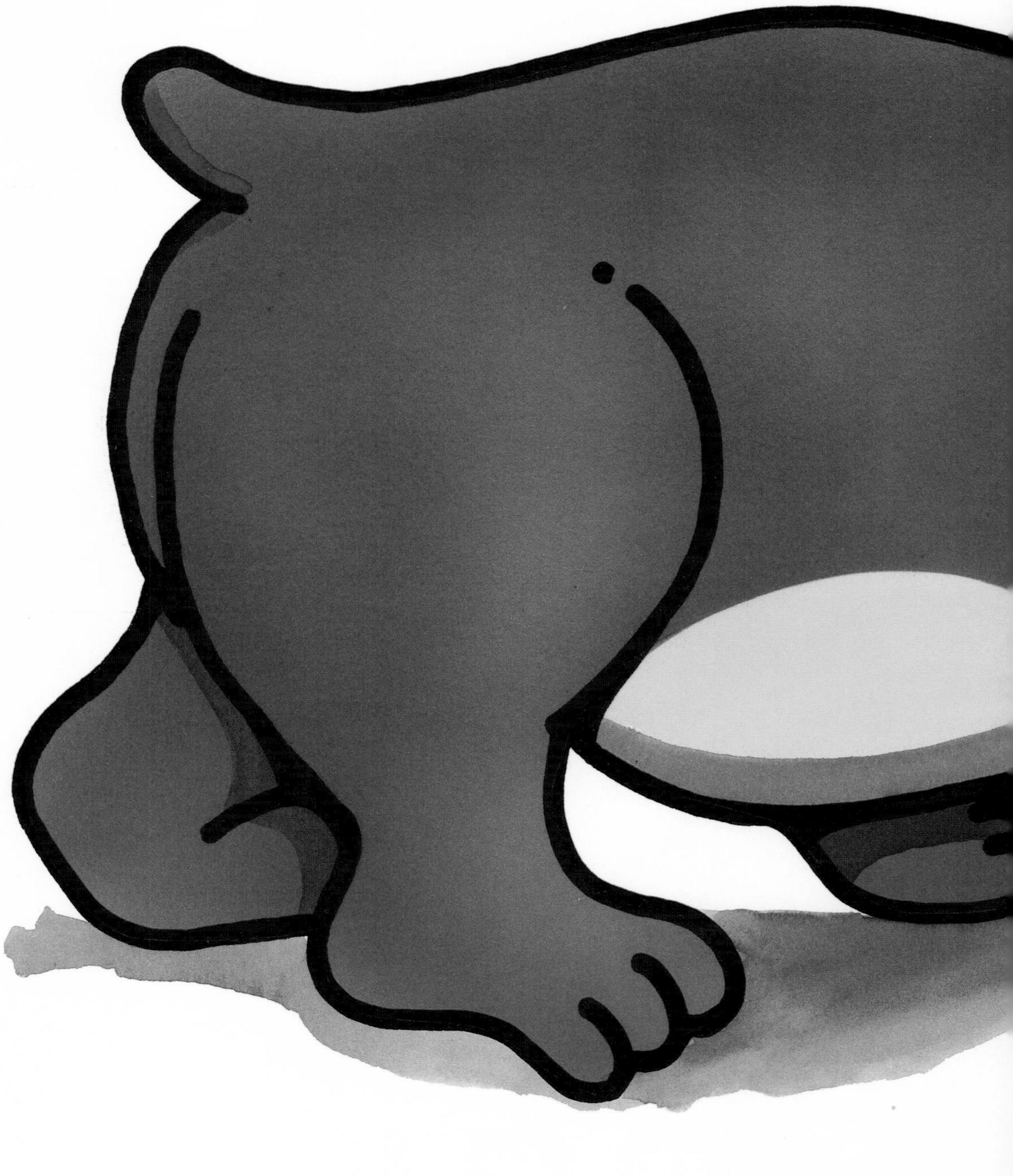

N

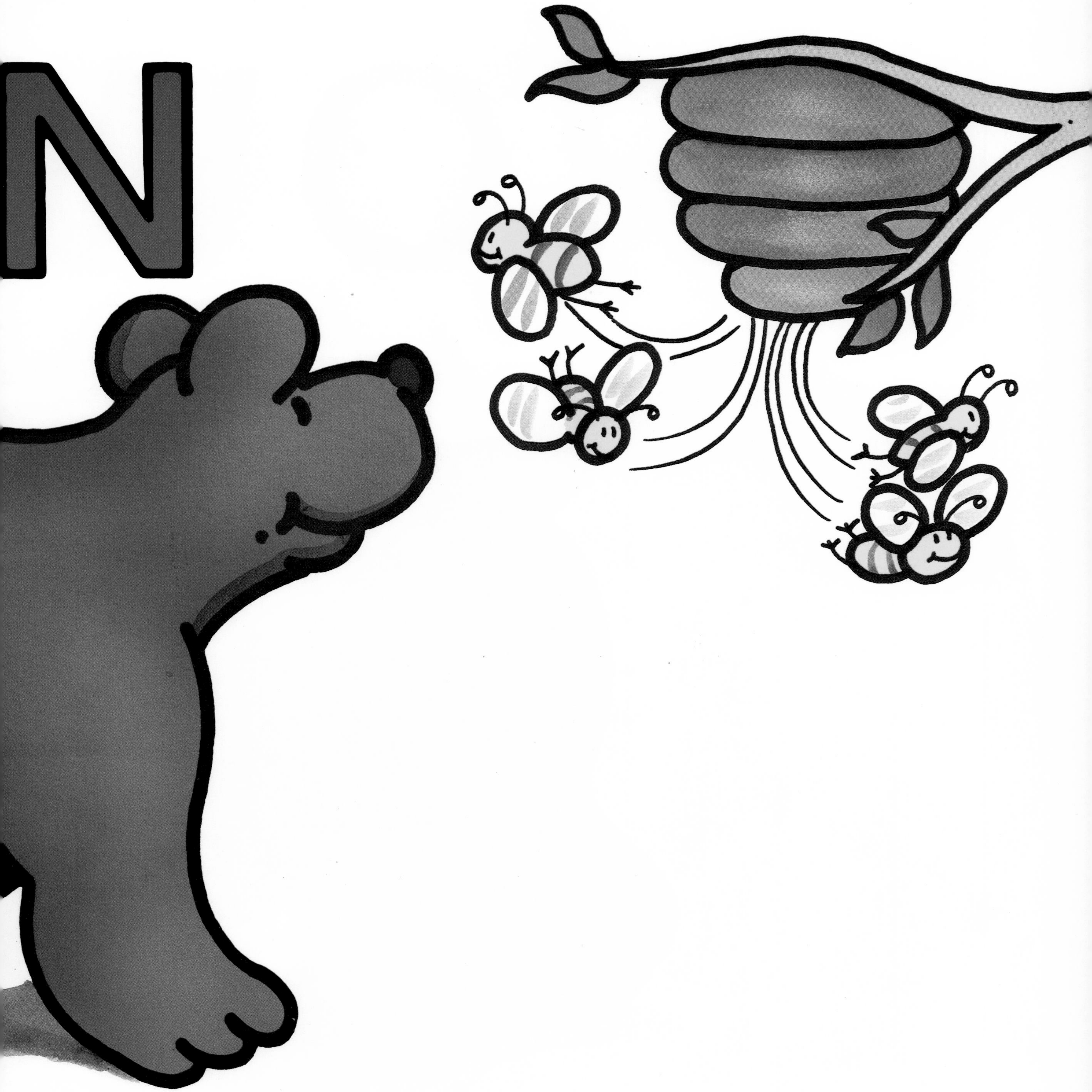

Bear

ORAN

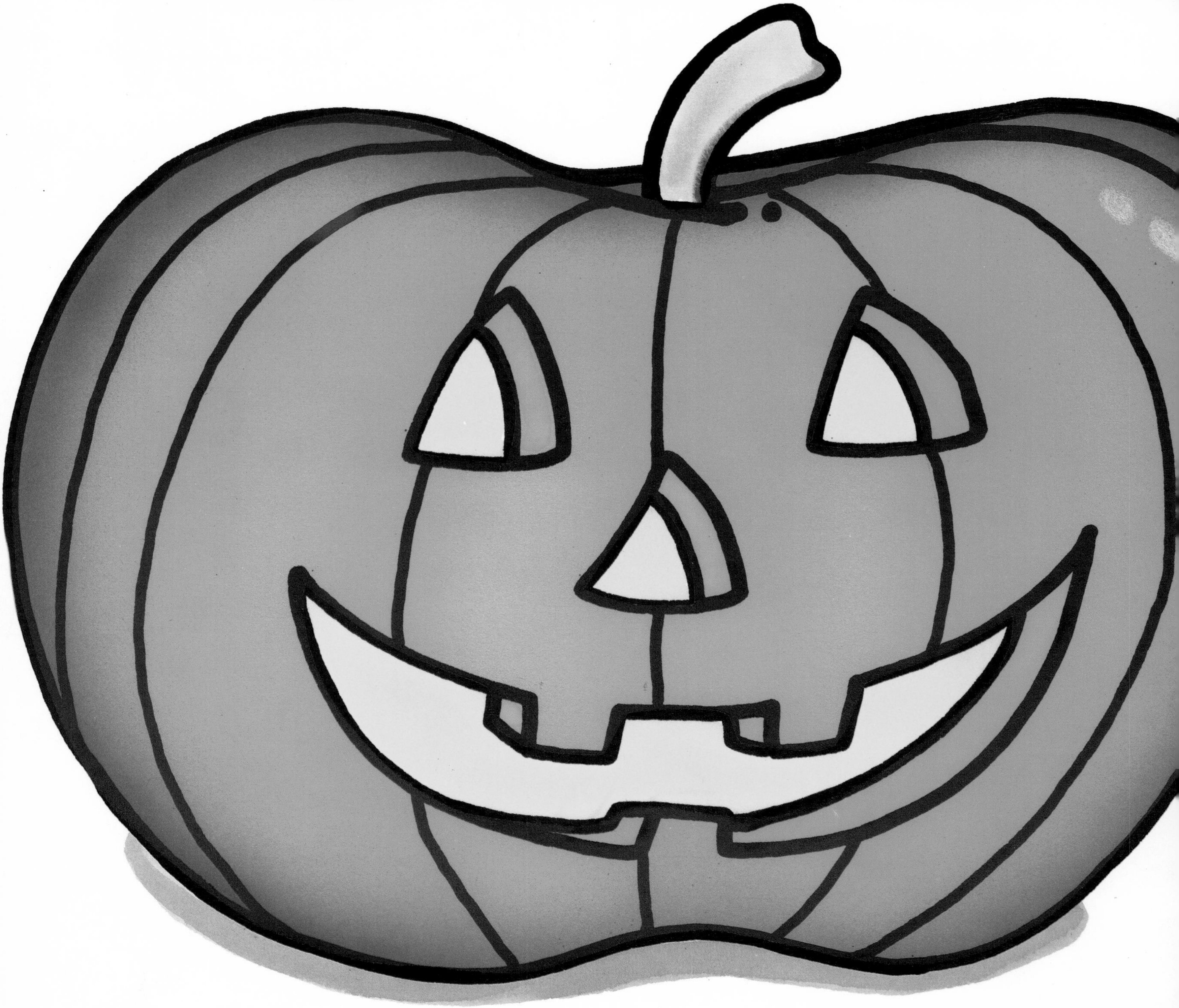

GE

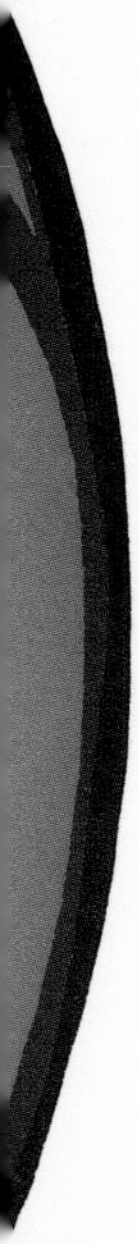

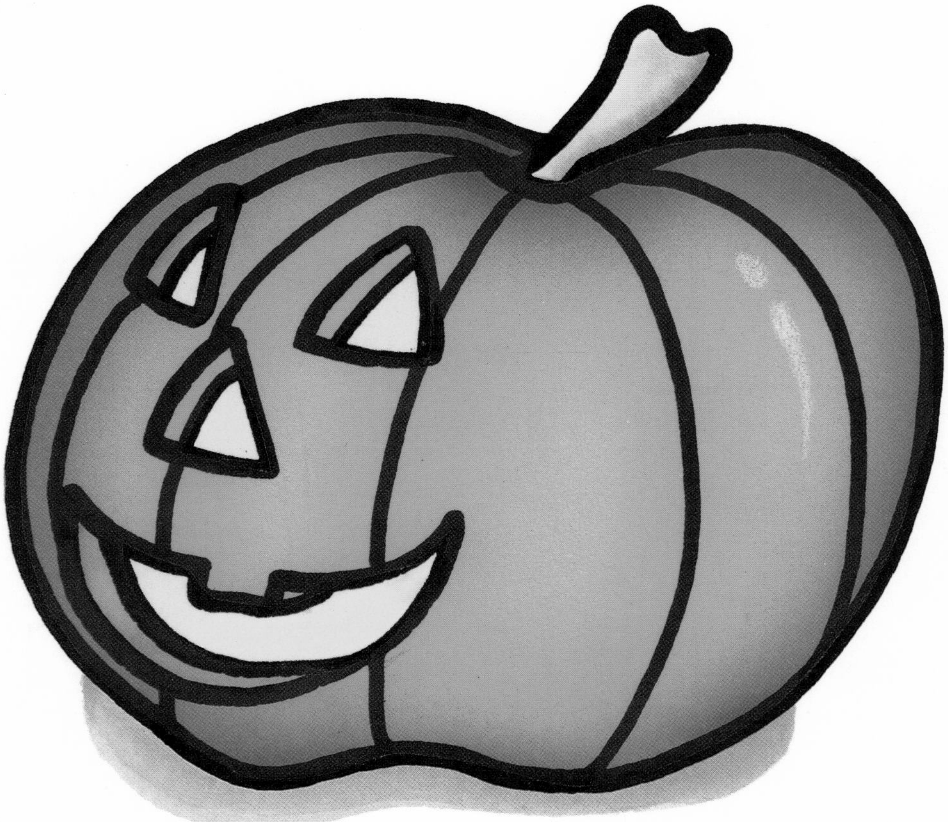

Pumpkins

WHITE

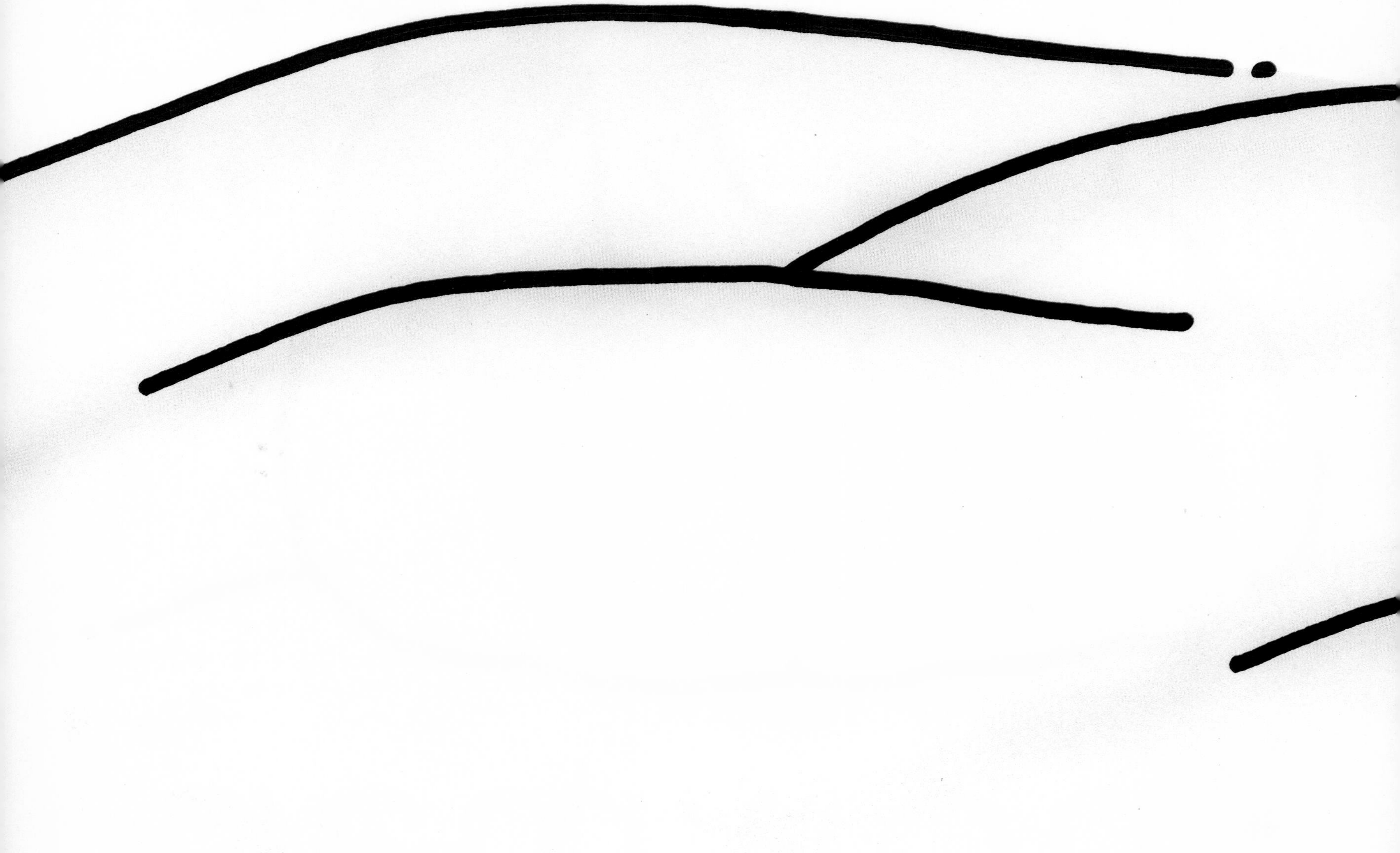

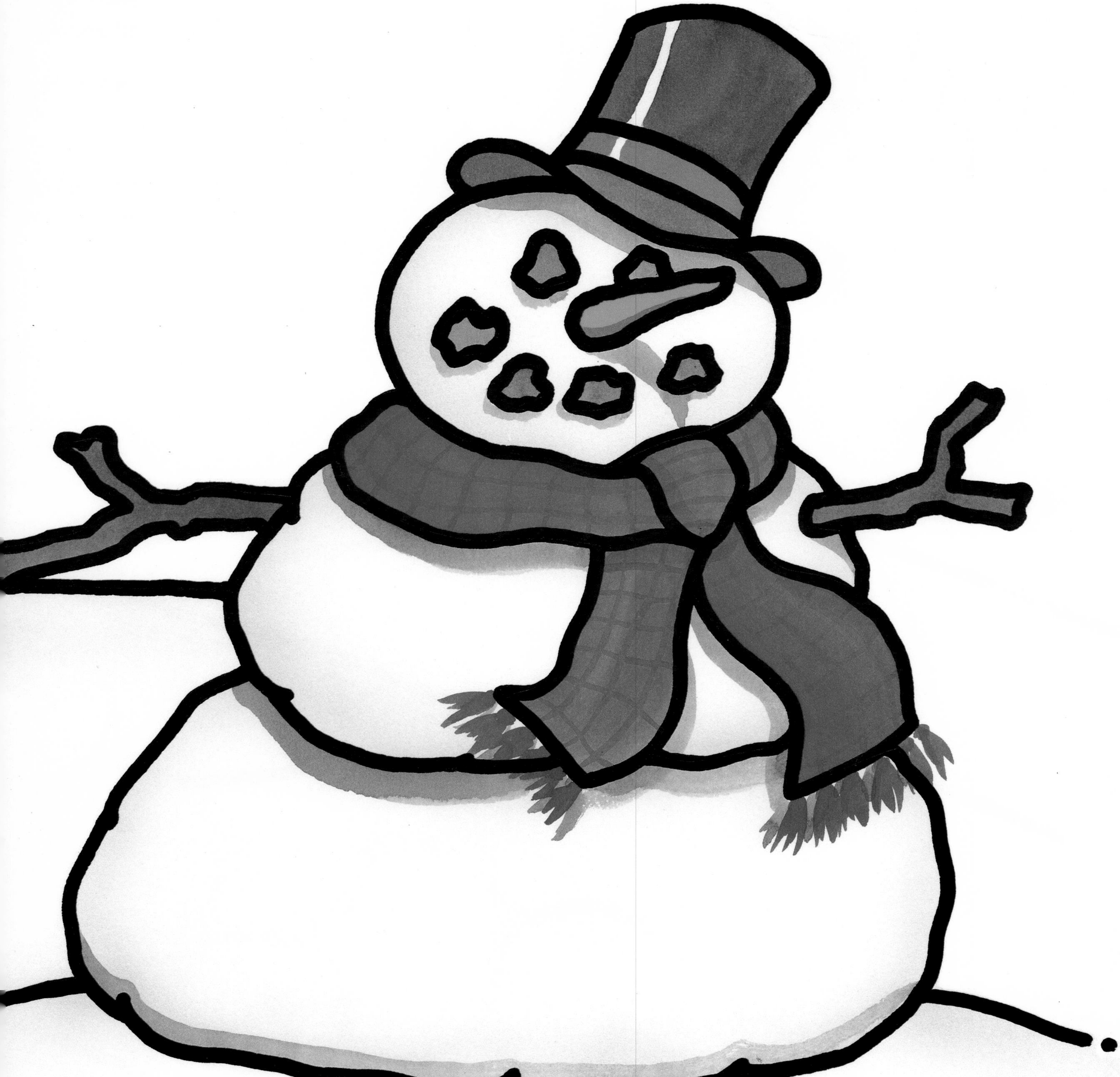

Snowman

PURPL

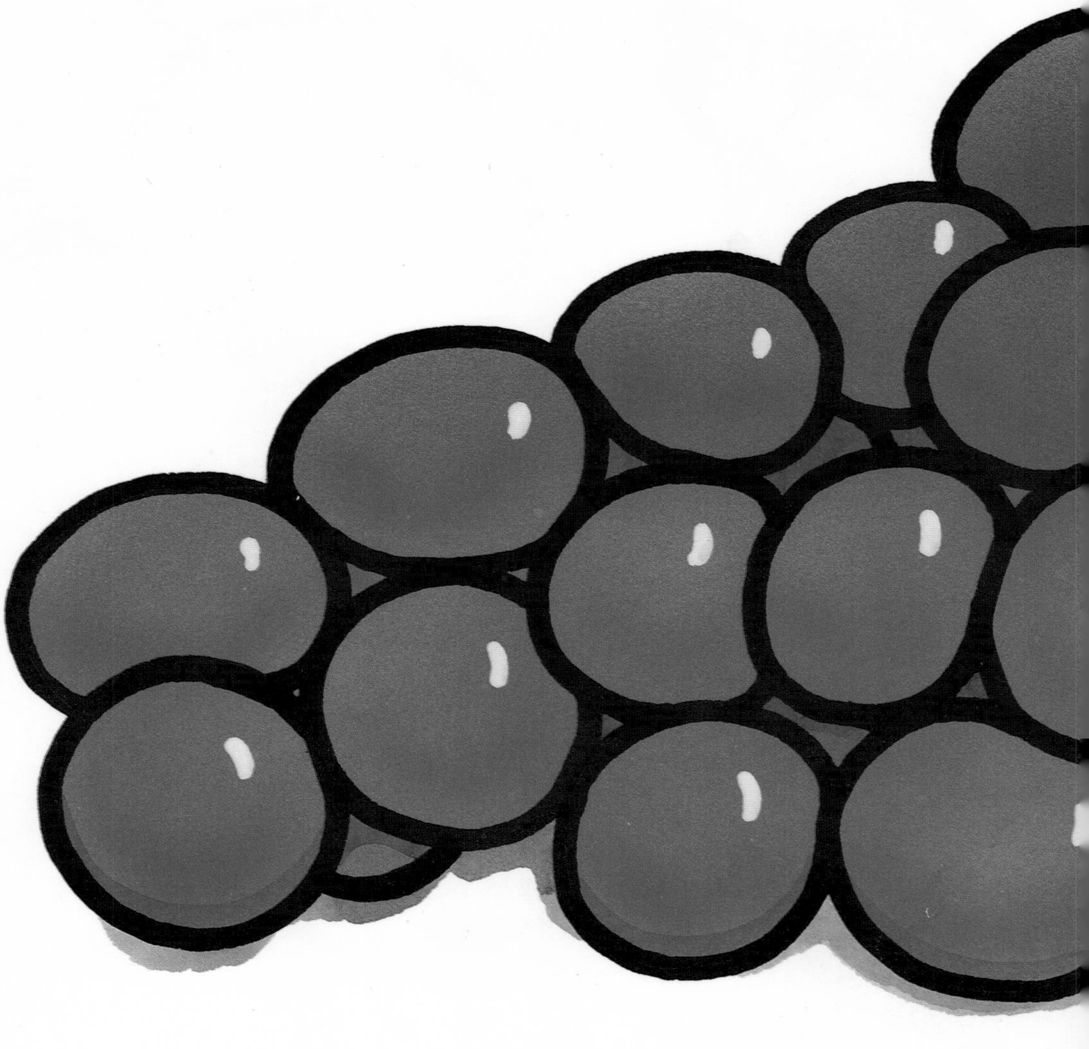

E

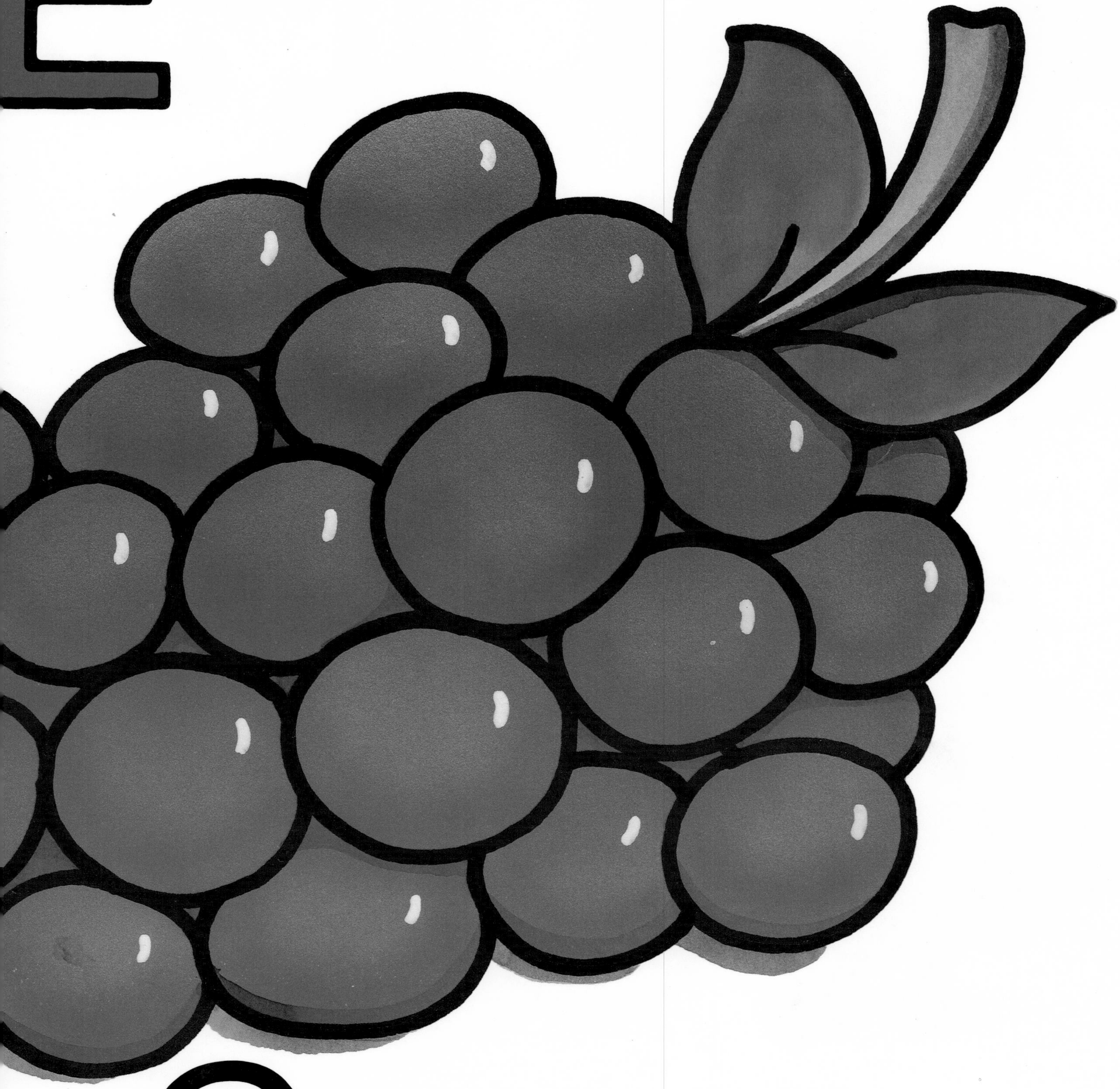

Grapes

YELLO

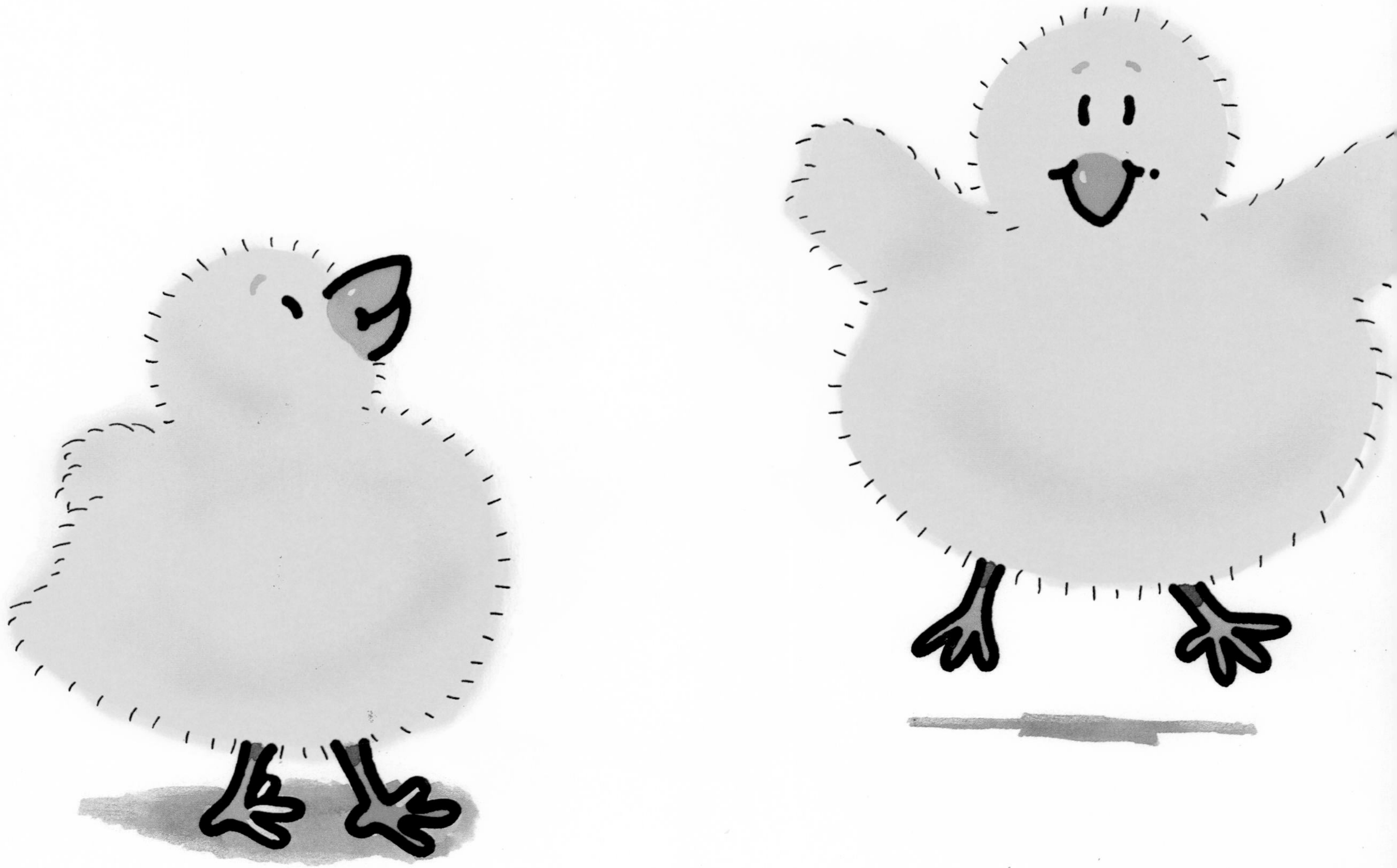

W

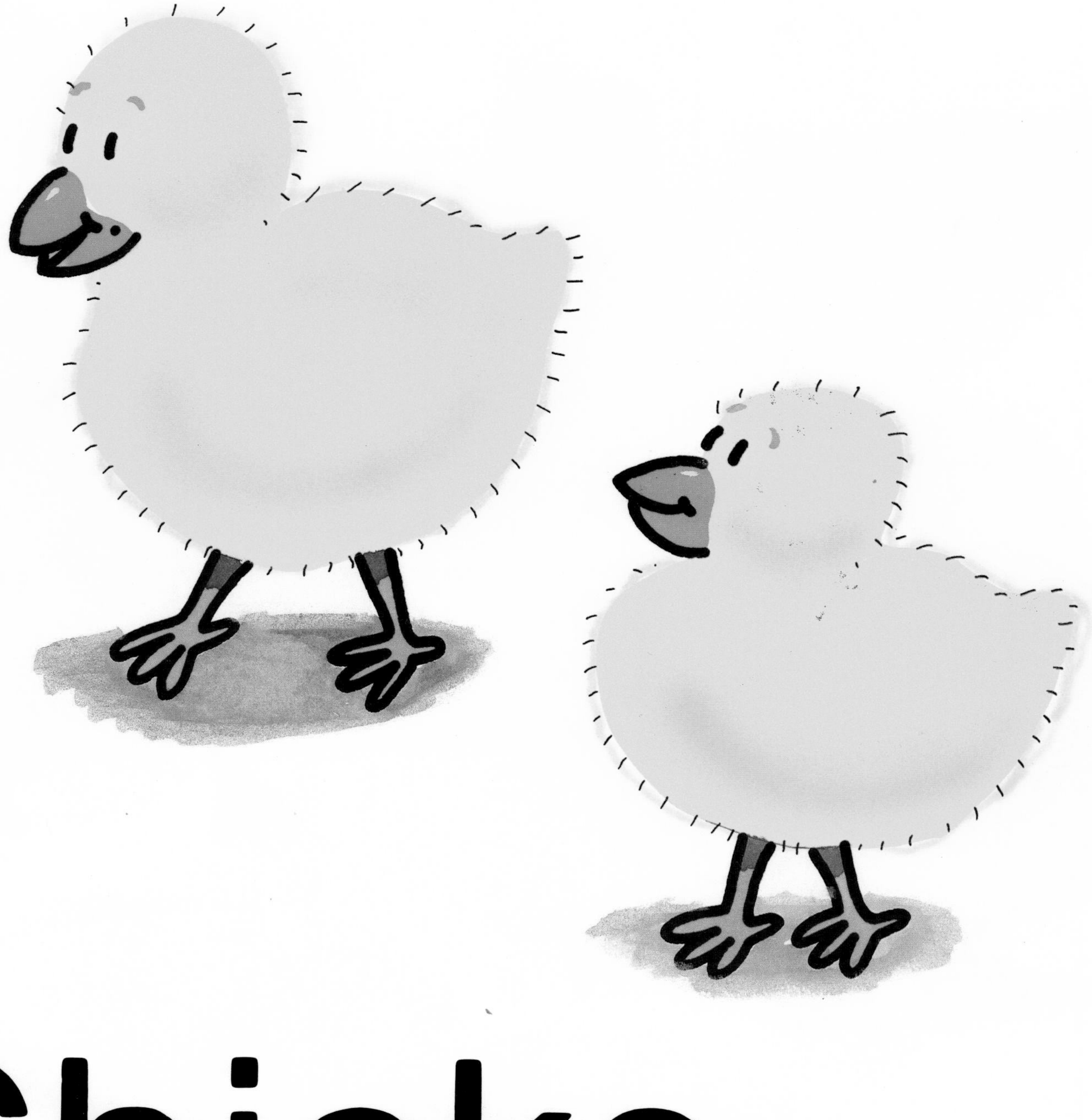

Chicks

BLACK

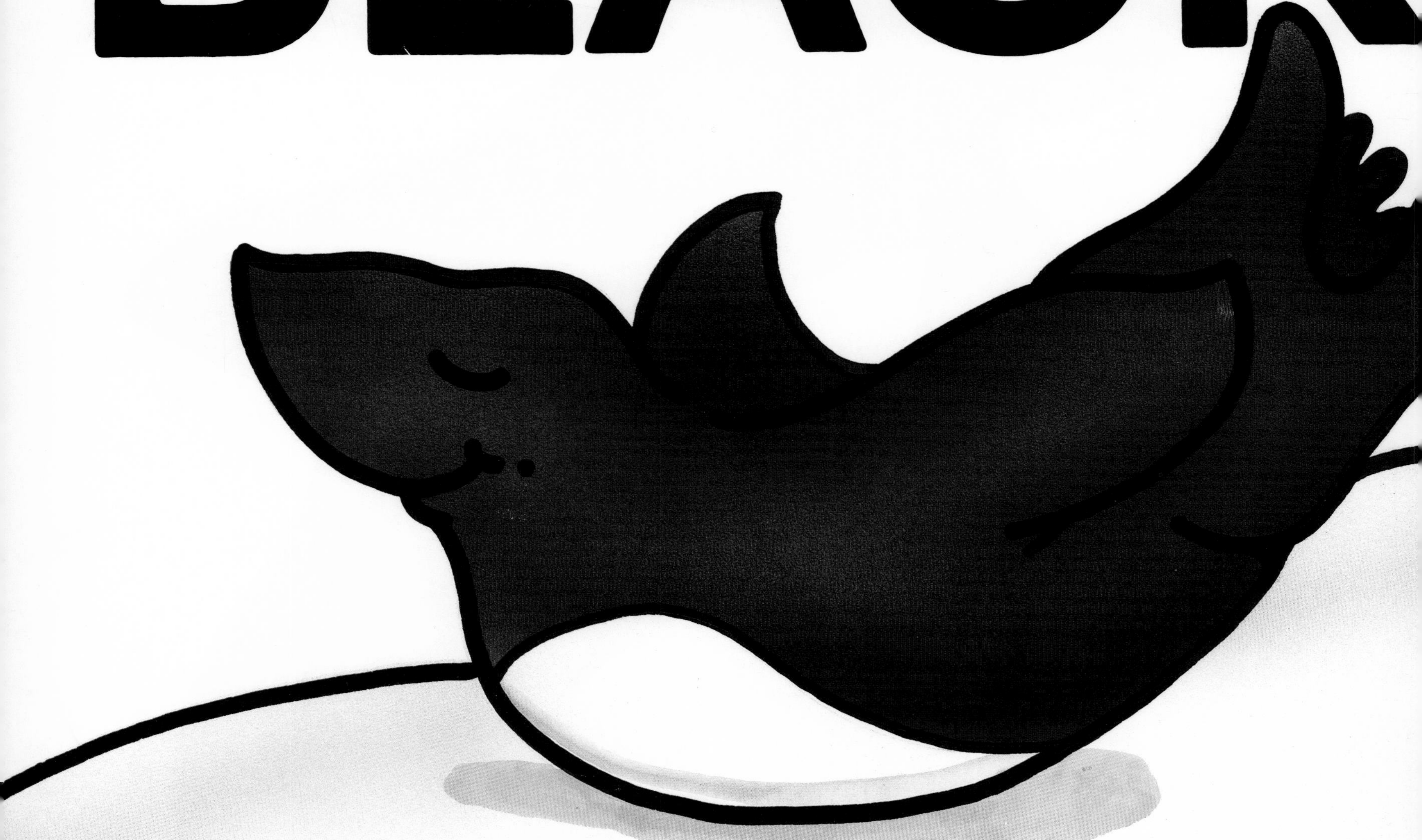

Pengu

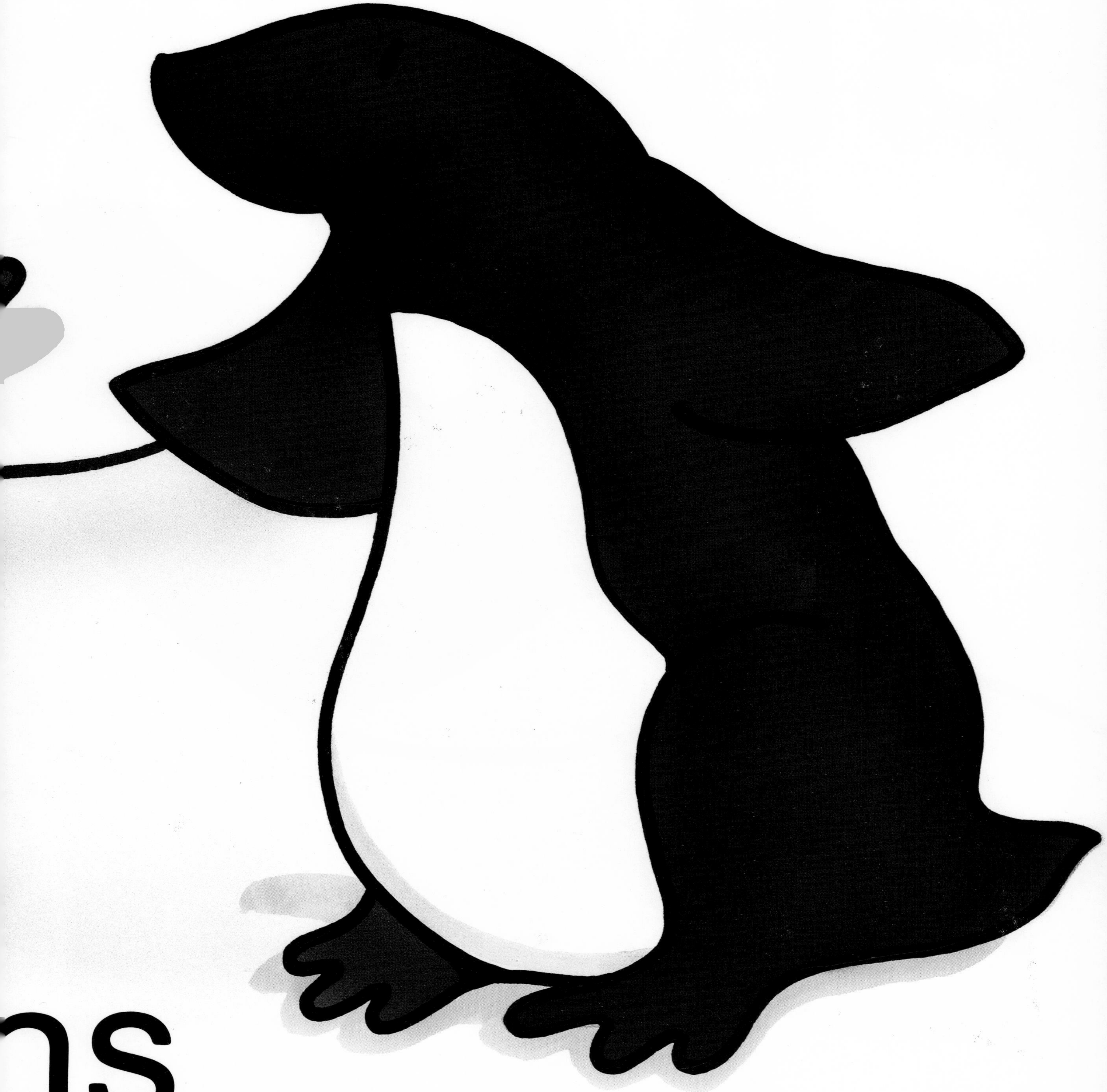

ns

GREEN

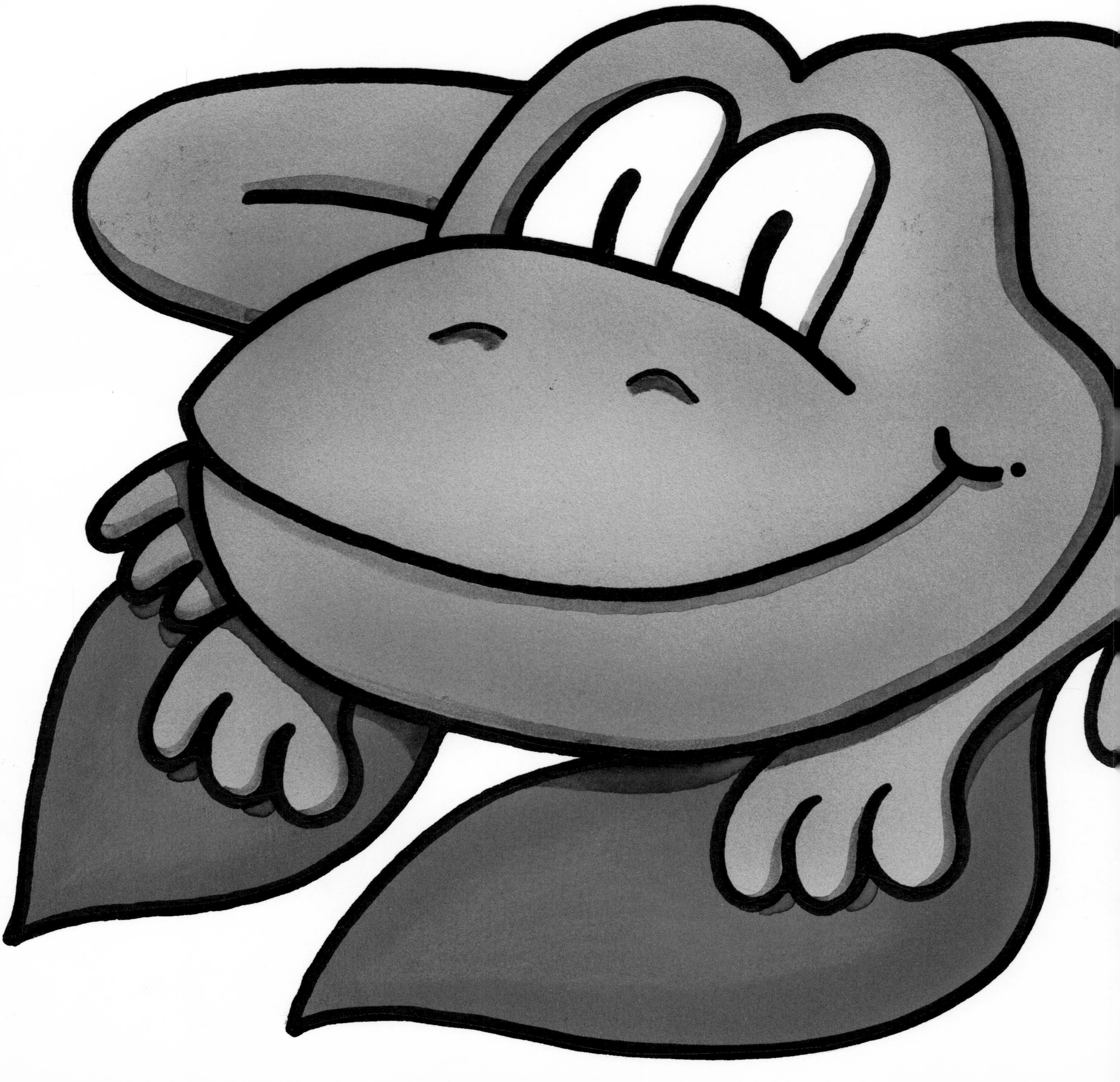

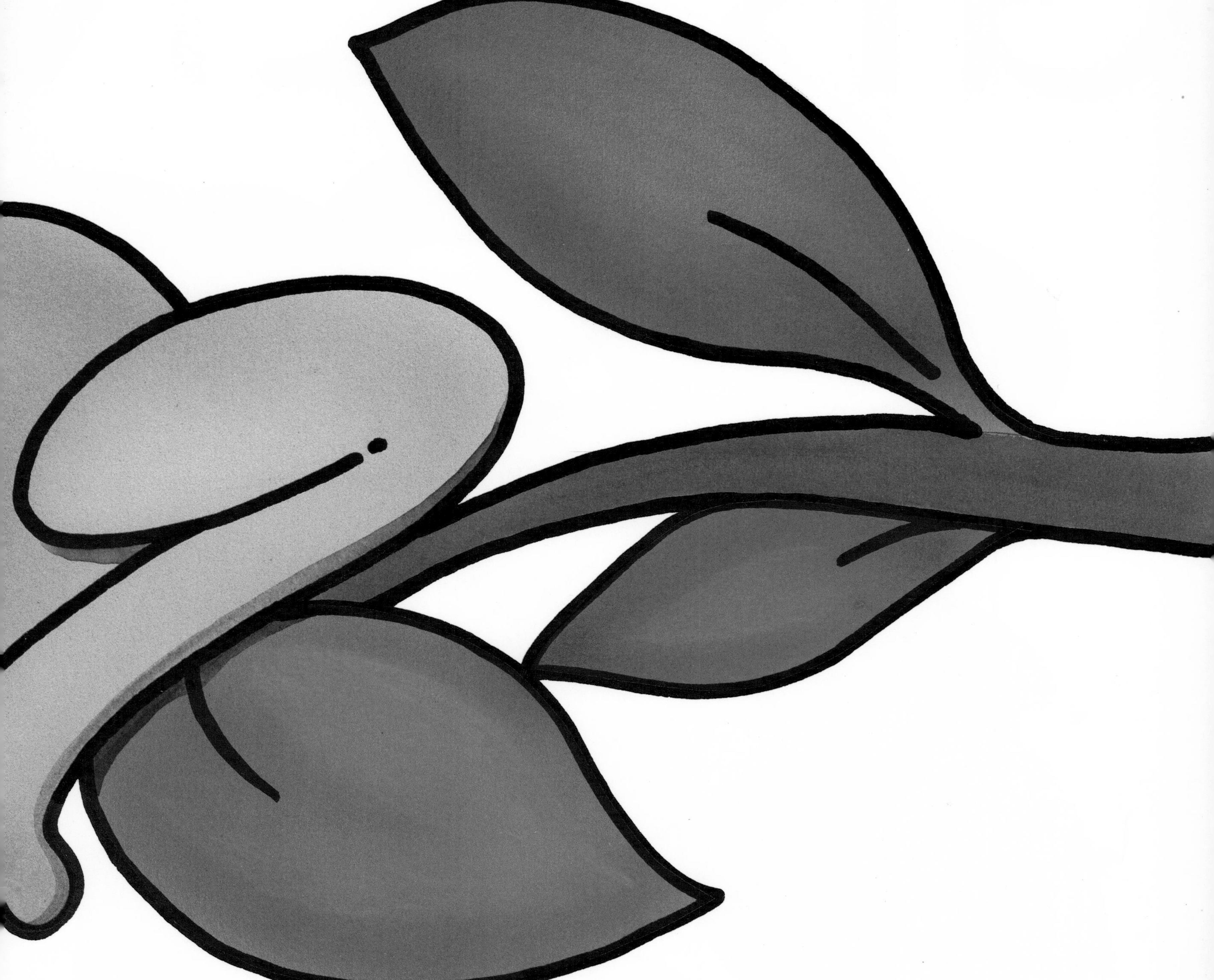

Frog

SILVER

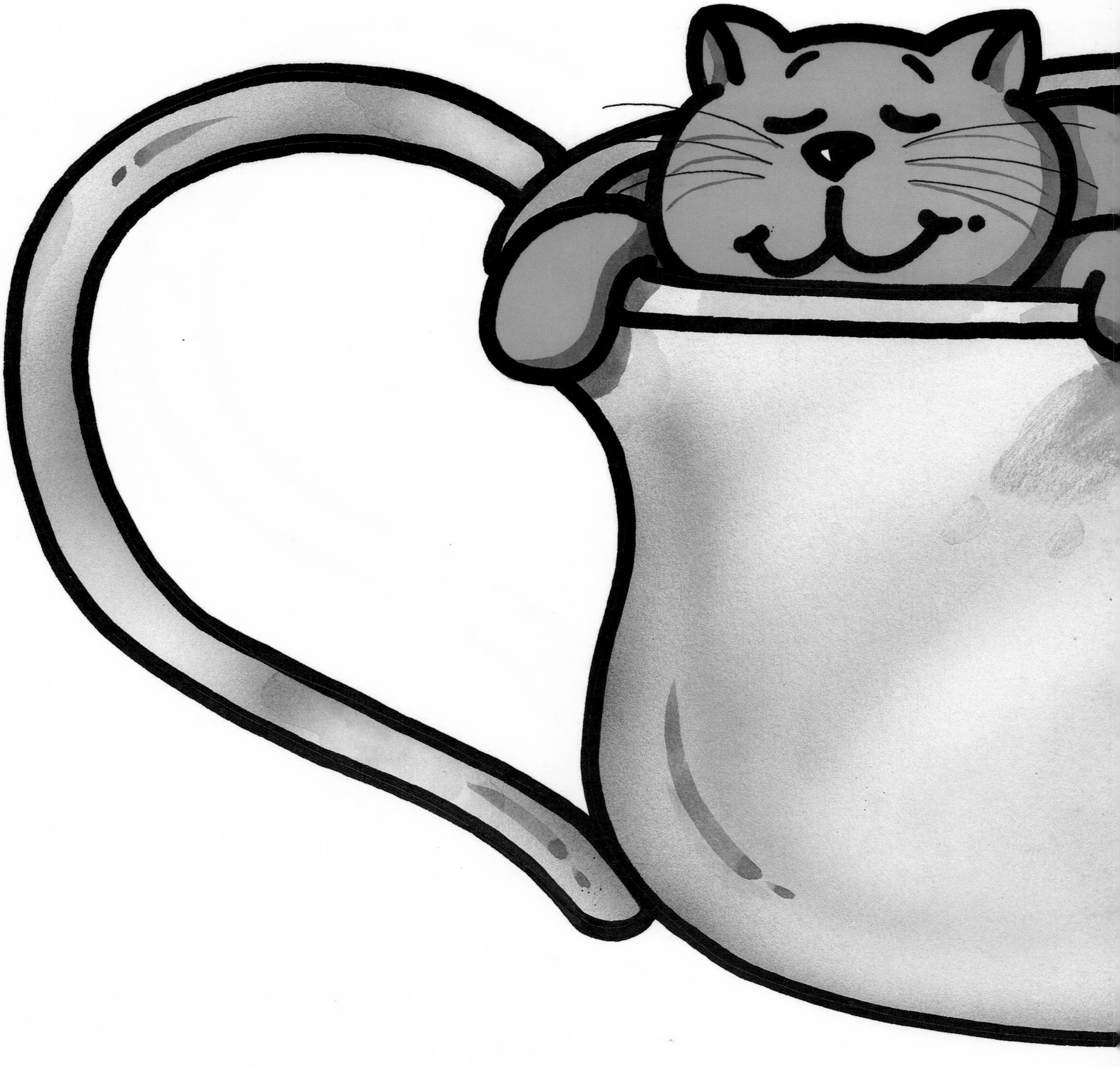